LET'S WRITE A SHORT STORY!

LET'S WRITE A SHORT STORY!

THE WRITE PRACTICE

with

JOE BUNTING

Hey Reader! Get a free 1-page download with the top 10 questions to make your story idea better here: https://thewritepractice.com/story-ideas-questions/

CONTENTS

MORE COMPETITIVE THAN HARVARD

If you google "Harvard Acceptance Rate," you'll find that in 2012, out of over 34,000 students who applied only 5.9 percent got in. Those are not great odds. Think of sixteen other people you know. If you all applied to Harvard, only one of you would get in, and it probably wouldn't be you. However, Harvard's acceptance rate is nothing compared to the top literary magazines.

The top literary magazines in America usually get about 1,000 submissions per month, 12,000 per year. A few submissions come from literary agents on behalf of the writers they work for, but most come from unknown or mostly unknown writers just trying to get their big break in the literary world. Of the estimated 12,000 submissions a magazine like *The New Yorker* gets per year, they pick only about 50. That's 0.4 percent.

To put that in perspective, think about 249 people you know. If all of you submitted to a literary magazine, only one of your stories would be accepted. And it almost certainly wouldn't be you.

It gets worse. Between July 2011 and July 2012, about 970

stories were submitted to *Glimmer Train Stories* by writers who use the popular submission tracking service, Duotrope. Only one was published. That's 0.1 percent.

Think about 1,000 people you know....

It's 50 times harder to get into *Glimmer Train* than it is to get into Harvard, according to Duotrope's stats.

No wonder writers have a reputation for being alcoholics. Who needs a drink after hearing that?

Not all literary magazines are this difficult. *Daily Science Fiction*, a popular online magazine that delivers a new science fiction or fantasy story to readers' inboxes every weekday, has an acceptance rate of a little more than 3 percent. However, of all the magazines I looked at as I researched this book, that was one of the highest. I hope you didn't think writing and publishing short stories was going to be easy.

Why Short Stories?

What do these stats tell you? If you want to get your short fiction published, not just in one magazine but to have pieces published in several of them, you need to get serious. You can break into the literary magazine scene, but it will take perseverance, hard work, and a little luck.

The reasons for writing short stories, though, make it well worth facing the obstacles. Here are eight:

1. Short Stories are Practice

How do you practice writing?

This was the question that led me to start The Write Practice in 2011. Learning experts like Geoffrey Colvin and Malcolm Gladwell say if you practice at a task deliberately, you will improve far more quickly than if you just perform the task for fun and with no forethought.

The Write Practice was my attempt to give writers a place to practice writing deliberately, for fifteen minutes a day, six times a week, and apparently it has hit a nerve. We've had hundreds of writers participate in our practicing community. I've talked to dozens of high profile people in the writing world about how to improve your writing through practice, including editors of some of the top literary magazines, creative writing professors, and even Pulitzer Prize winning authors. All of this has led me to the conclusion that one of the best ways to improve at the craft of writing is by writing short stories.

To practice writing deliberately you have to write finished pieces over and over again. Writing finished pieces can motivate you to persevere through the moments when writing itself is difficult. Deliberate practice is often unsatisfying. To improve, it's helpful to have the reward of a finished piece and the chance of publication to motivate you through writer's block.[1]

Even more importantly, to practice deliberately you have to put your writing skills to the test. Researchers as early as the 1890s have found that when people are tested, they improve significantly, even people with years of experience at a task.[2] Compare that to how you write. Too many of us write whatever we feel like, and then wonder why we're not getting better (or worse, why others aren't responding to our "art"). It's fine to write as a hobby. Writing is fun. However, if you just write what you feel like you will improve a lot slower than you will if you "test" yourself by constantly submitting your work for publication.

You can write novels and publish novels to "test" yourself, but novels (obviously) take a lot longer to write than short stories. That's why MFA writing programs across the country rely on short stories as deliberate practice for writing fiction.

If you want to get better at writing fiction, write and submit a lot of short stories.

2. *Short Stories Allow You to Fail Faster*

I once wrote a short story that I thought was the best piece of literature since *The Brothers Karamozov*. I thought magazines would beg me to publish my story. I sent it to five of them, and they all rejected it. I sent the story to five more. I received five more rejection slips. I used the rejection slips as coasters and tried to spill as much coffee as I could on them. A year later, I finally realized the story wasn't any good.

All the writers I know have had their work rejected, from Stephen King to J.K. Rowling to my chiropractor who writes novels in his spare time. If you want to be a writer, expect rejection. It's actually a badge of honor.

The benefit of writing short stories is that they allow you to get rejected sooner. If you write a novel, it could take years for your work to be rejected. With short stories, you could be rejected in weeks. Rejection is the best teacher you can have. You will learn more about writing from having your work rejected than from a years' worth of writing courses.

As John Keats said, "Failure is, in a sense, the highway to success, inasmuch as every discovery of what is false leads us to seek earnestly after what is true, and every fresh experience points out some form of error which we shall afterwards carefully avoid."

3. Short Stories Can Make Your Career

The rewards for publishing in a leading literary magazine are huge. "Agents look to literary magazines to find talented emerging writers," Linda Swanson-Davies, editor of *Glimmer Train*, told me. "Their plates are full, too. It's helpful to be able to read a collection of stories vetted by editors whose taste and opinions they respect. After each issue of Glimmer Train comes out, we are contacted by agents who've read stories they loved and are interested in representing the authors. If your goal is to publish a book, having first published fiction in literary magazines gives publishers more confidence in the merit and marketability of an author's work."

Is it necessary to get published in a literary magazine to get a book deal? I asked a best-selling, Pulitzer Prize winning author this question off the record, and he told me that no, it's not necessary. It is, however, a great way to build your career. If your story is published by *The New Yorker* or one of the other big literary magazines, you're going to make it much more difficult for an agent or a publisher to reject your manuscript. Even publishing a story in smaller, obscure magazines shows publishers that you have experience and know how the publishing process works.

4. Short Stories Can Make You Feel Warm and Fuzzy

On top of the benefits to your career, having an editor who reads thousands of short stories per year say they love your work enough to publish it is a pretty good feeling. Imagine getting that letter or email and being able to tell all your friends and family you are now a published author. Imagine seeing your name in print for the first time, smelling the pages of the magazine, and knowing thousands of readers are reading your story at the same time. Would that be worth it to you?

5. Short Stories Can Get You Paid

You can even earn money writing short stories. Many magazines pay writers when they accept their short stories, and it's always nice to get paid for doing what you love. On top of that, whether you want to publish them in a literary magazine or not, in the age of self-publishing you can turn your short stories into ebooks and sell them on Amazon or through your personal website.

6. Short Stories are Recycling

Short stories don't necessarily have to be written from scratch. If you're like me, you have a couple of half-finished novels collecting digital dust somewhere on your hard drive. Why not turn them into short stories? After a little editing, you can send them to literary magazines. You might make some money, build your audience, and recycle your old work all at once.

We'll talk about this more in the chapter, How to Make Twice as Much on Your Short Story.

7. They're Research

In 1925, Ernest Hemingway published his first book entitled *In Our Time*, a collection of short stories primarily about a young man named Nick Adams. In the next years, Hemingway would write over twenty stories involving Adams. He would become the prototypical Hemingway hero: courageous, stoic, and consumed by complicated relationships with women.

The remarkable thing is that nearly every protagonist Hemingway created has roots in Nick Adams. In other words, the Nick Adams short stories were research. By looking at one character from so many different settings and situations, Hemingway was able to "observe" him, to understand him, and to translate him into Jake Barnes, the protagonist of *The Sun Also Rises*, into Robert Jordan, from *For Whom the Bell Tolls*, and even into Santiago, the old man *in The Old Man and the Sea*.

If you want to develop deep, complex, vivid characters, the short story could be a good laboratory to experiment with them.

8. Because You Are a Writer

The best reason to write short stories is because you are a writer. You open up new worlds for your readers. You create intriguing, heroic, despicable, beautiful characters. You tell stories that connect your readers to the rest of humanity, that connect them to their souls.

The short story is one of the oldest art forms in the world. People were telling short stories around the campfire long before they had the means of writing them down. Short stories are told every day all over the world. The amazing thing is that you get to write them down. That is your great privilege as a writer, to capture the world's stories and put them in a form that can be shared around the world.

Who Is This Book For?

I just want to help you write short stories.

This book could be read in a single sitting on a Saturday afternoon, and yet the tools here will help you launch your career, become a better writer, and take the small, practical steps toward publication. Most people don't know how short stories work. They don't know how to write them, how they're different from novels, how to structure them, and once they're written, how to get them published. This book will remove much of that mystery.

If you're reading this book I want you to promise me something. You have to promise to write and submit a short story to a literary magazine.

Are you ready to make that promise to me and to yourself? That this book won't just be a little bit of interesting information, but that you will apply it? That immediately after reading this, you'll get to work on a short story, maybe your first? If you're ready to make that promise, get accountability. If you have a blog, write a post titled "Let's Write a Short Story!" and share your plan to write a short story by the end of the month (if you do, email me and I'll share it: joe@thewritepractice.com). Go on Facebook or Twitter and tell the world, "This month, I'm going to write a short story." If you want, you can use the hashtag #thewritepractice so we can see it.

If you can't make that promise, then this book isn't for you. I would rather you put it down right now. But if you're ready to improve at the craft of writing, kick off your career, impress agents, dive into new characters, and do what you love—write—then let's write a short story.

1

LET'S GET STARTED

If you haven't read many short stories, you may be wondering, "What is a short story?" This is as difficult a question to answer as, "What is a novel?" Short stories take many forms, both in traditional and experimental literature. On top of that, each genre (science fiction, romance, literary) has a different style and feel for their short stories. However, below are three observations of how they usually look.

Short Stories Are Short

While length isn't the only way to define short stories, it's probably the simplest. The classic definition of a short story is a work of fiction that's longer than 1,000 words and shorter than 20,000.[3]

If you'd like to write stories shorter than 1,000 words (about three pages), then you're writing flash fiction. There are magazines that publish flash fiction, and you can find a list of nine to start with in Appendix A.

If your story is longer than 20,000 words, it would be

considered a novella. If it's over 40,000 words, it's probably a novel.

Even though short stories can be up to 20,000 words long, most of those published in literary magazines today are between 3,000 and 5,000. For example, the popular literary journal *Ploughshares* says in their guidelines, "General submissions of prose can run up to approximately 6,000 words, although space constraints often mean we prefer prose pieces around 5,000 words." If you want to have the best chance to publish your short story, aim for 3,000 to 5,000 words.

Short Stories Are Stories

This may seem obvious, but sometimes the short stories people write aren't very good stories. Donald Miller says, "A story is a character who wants something and overcomes conflict to get it." Another way to define story is, a character who has a problem, fails repeatedly at solving that problem, and then either succeeds or fails at solving it. A third definition is, a character who experiences an event that changes her forever.

These are rough generalizations, but I think they reveal five things about what makes a good story:

- **A Character.** William Faulkner said about writing stories, "It begins with a character, usually, and once he stands up on his feet and begins to move, all I can do is trot along behind him with a paper and pencil trying to keep up long enough to put down what he says and does." Stories are about people, not ideas, not even events. If you're not writing about a person, you're not writing a short story.

- **Desire + A Decision.** Your characters must want something (or *not* want something), preferably something great. But more than that, they must be willing to take action to get what they want. Characters who idly watch their lives go by are not protagonists. They are background characters. Does your protagonist make a decision?
- **Conflict.** Good stories have powerful bad guys, whether the bad guy is external: a person, a group of people, or nature; or internal: a belief or side of the protagonist's personality.
- **Change.** Why do you need conflict? Because people only change when they experience pain, and all stories involve transformation. Joy, unfortunately, is a lousy teacher. Don't be nice to your characters. It won't help your story. Pain creates transformation.
- **Resolution.** Do your characters solve their problems or do they fail? Do they get what they want or not? You need to show this. Don't end your story too soon. Sit with your characters while they enjoy their success or wallow in their failure for a moment. Editors say bad endings are one of the biggest reasons they reject stories. Readers need resolution.

Short Stories Involve a Major Event

Think about some of your favorite characters in novels. For me, there's John Grady Cole from *All the Pretty Horses*, Mr. Darcy from *Pride and Prejudice*, the old man from *The Old Man and the Sea*, Jean Valjean from *Les Miserables*, and Alyosha from *The Brother's Karamazov*, among many others. Now, think of your favorite characters from short stories, if you've read many. What are their names? Can't think of them? You might be able to think of a few events or characteristics from your favorite short stories, but I doubt you'll be able to remember many names.

Besides length, one of the major things distinguishing short stories from other literary forms is they usually feature one major event. In this way, short stories are event-driven rather than character-driven. I'm not saying short stories can't involve deep, complicated characters with realistic lives. I also don't mean that the characters don't dictate the story. Instead, I mean that the structure of short stories typically focuses on one major event, and it's easier to remember the event rather than the character.

There are certainly exceptions to this. For example, the celebrated author Denis Johnson writes short stories that often jump from event to event like montages. His stories are fantastical journeys rather than slow build ups to a central event. However, even his stories seem to contain a defining moment that focuses the story.

Short Stories Feature One Important Character

Clearly, short stories aren't long, and while you have room to explore five or six important characters in a novel, short stories generally focus on just one. That being said, you can go to great depths exploring that one character that you do focus on. Feel free to have her make bad decisions and have to retrace her steps to make things right. Have her reject the call to action several times before finally accepting. Allow her to try and fail and try and fail and try again only to fail or succeed (your choice!). She can be a femme fatale who does good things or a goody girl who does bad things. The short story form gives you freedom to explore the heights and depths of your characters.

In fact, this is what makes short stories so important for writers working on their craft. If you eventually want to write novels, the short story allows you to explore individual characters' actions, history, and motivations in a more focused way than you can achieve with a novel.

The rest of the characters in your short stories shouldn't compete with your protagonist for attention. If you have too many complex characters, you will have a hard time fitting them all into the limited structure. Your story may also feel too busy and chaotic. In every story, whether a novel, a film, or a short story, your main characters must go through a life-altering transformation. In a short story, there's no time for more than one or two characters to go through that change.

Instead, just pick one hero or heroine you're going to stick with.

Can You Break the Rules?

If these characteristics rile up your rule-breaking tendencies, that's great! All of these "rules" can be and have been broken, and if you're so inspired, you can find new ways to break each of them. As Keith Jennings says, one of the most exciting parts of the creative process is breaking the rules and coloring outside of the lines. Let these guidelines act as the lines in a coloring book. Then go color outside the lines as much as you want.

What a Short Story is Not

In addition to defining what a short story is, I think it's helpful to talk about what they are not. Here are three things they are not:

Short Stories Do Not Have Subplots

Novels often have multiple stories that diverge from the main story. These divergent stories are called subplots. For example, in *Pride and Prejudice*, the main plot follows Elizabeth Bennet and Mr. Darcy as they move from initial dislike for each other to passionate love. One of the subplots, then, is Jane's relationship with Mr. Bingley as they go from mutual interest to unexplained rejection to marriage. While Elizabeth is intimately involved in Jane and Mr. Bingley's courtship, this subplot is not the center of the story. In fact, much as we like Jane and Mr. Bingley, you could remove the subplot and the story would still work—as Helen Fielding showed us with *Bridget Jones Diary*, based on *Pride and Prejudice*.

Short stories, however, do not have subplots. There's just no room for them. Instead, there is just one plot leading to one major event or climactic moment.

They Are Not Poems

While short stories can be written poetically, at their heart they are not poems. Short stories contain, as their name implies, a story. Poetry doesn't have that same burden, and although epic poetry was the first form of written storytelling, most modern poetry today focuses on an image, idea, or mood rather than a story.

They Are Not Plotless

Thus, short stories are not plotless. Short stories have elements of plot—an inciting incident, dark night of the soul, climax, and resolution. However, because of their compressed form, they won't necessarily have all the elements of plot. This is why novelists can often turn their individual chapters into short stories. There still has to be plot, but you don't necessarily need that much.

We'll cover what you do need and what you can do without in the Story Structure section.

Now that you have an idea about what a short story is, let's get started learning how to write and publish them.

How Do You Get Published by Literary Magazines

One of the things you'll hear most from literary magazines is to understand whether your story fits their magazine you have to actually read the magazine.

It makes sense. Before you write, you should read. And each magazine has their own unique style, their own list of criteria that they're looking for. In fact, here are several magazines saying just this:

> A general familiarity with what we have published in the past is the best guide to our needs and preferences.
>
> — *The Atlantic*

> To read *PANK* is to know *PANK*. To read a lot within the literary magazine and small press universe (there's plenty to choose from) is to know *PANK*. Unfortunately, we see a lot of submissions from writers who clearly aren't reading

much of anything. Serious writers are serious readers. Read. Seriously.

— *PANK*

We recommend that you read a copy of the journal before sending your work for consideration so that you can see if your writing and *Crazyhorse* are a good match.

— *Crazyhorse*

Our criteria for publication are best gauged by a close reading of the magazine.

— *Granta*

We ask those who wish to submit writing—whether fiction, essay, interview, memoir or poetry—to read the journal and get an idea for the type and range of material we publish.

— *Image*

Please read the magazine before submitting. Much of the nonfiction we receive indicates very clearly the submitter has never looked at the magazine.

— *Virginia Quarterly Review*

The best, really the only, way to get an idea of our editorial tastes and policies vis a vis styles of writing we admire is to read past issues of the magazine.

— FENCE

Reading the magazine before submitting sounds obvious. However, this isn't as easy as the magazines would like you to believe.

There are thousands of literary magazines out there, and while some of them are available for free online, many are not. This means you have to buy copies at $8-$15 a piece, sometimes for a magazine that may not match your style. You could spend hundreds of dollars and dozens of hours, just on finding the right place to send your work, work that, let's not forget, has only a fraction of a chance of being chosen anyway.

It's exhausting to think about, isn't it?

In the years since I started submitting to magazines—and hearing the above advice from the same magazines that ended up rejecting me—I've found some tricks to save all that time and money and still get the knowledge you need to send your story to the right place.

Here are six pieces of advice:

1. Ask your friends.

Just because you haven't read any literary magazines doesn't mean other writers you know haven't. Before I ever submit a short story, I ask a few of my writer friends where they think I should send it. Sometimes, this is even better because other people are better judges of your work than you are. They might be able to see where it fits even if you can't.

2. Team up with other writers.

To take that advice to the next level, if you know writers who are also trying to get published in literary magazines, help each other out. Each person can subscribe to and study one literary magazine. Then, report to each other about the magazine's unique style.

If you don't have a group of writing friends you can do this with, check out the community we're launching, Let's Write a Short Story (letswriteashortstory.com), where you can find an ever-growing list of literary magazines with notes from other writers.

3. Go to the library.

Most libraries subscribe to dozens of literary magazines and store them for years. You usually can't take them home, but you can go with a notepad and pen and spend a Saturday afternoon studying each magazine for their unique style.

4. Read Yearly Collections.

Every year, anthologies are published that host the best short stories of the year. The major ones are *The Best American Short Stories*, *The Pushcart Prize: Best of the Small* Presses, and *The Pen / O. Henry Prize* for literary short stories, and for fantasy / sci-fi, *The Year's Best Science Fiction & Fantasy*, *The Best Science Fiction and Fantasy of the Year*, and *The Year's Best SF*.[4] Creative titles. I know.

Not only will these anthologies help you discover the best stories in your genre, they will also help you familiarize yourself with the magazines that publish the prize-winning pieces.

5. Read online.

While there are still some magazines that don't have content available on their website, thousands either publish their entire magazine digitally or carry sample work online. We've included a list of magazines in Appendix A with links to their websites. That would be a great place to start.

6. Submit everywhere.

While this isn't the most efficient way to handle things,

you can also just submit your story everywhere, even if you're not sure whether it fits or not. This is kind of like playing the numbers game when you're applying for a job. Eventually your story might be accepted somewhere, but it takes a lot of work and creates a lot of waste for everyone involved. I recommend against this strategy.

Two Types of Submissions

While you're researching magazines, it's essential to look at their submission guidelines. These are usually on their website, and they tell you more about what each magazine is looking for, when and how to send them your manuscripts, and what subjects they accept. It's important to pay close attention to each magazine's guidelines. If you don't follow them, many will throw your manuscript out without reading it.

However, let's focus on one aspect you might find in the guidelines: themed submissions. There are two types of literary magazines, as they relate to the writer. There are magazines that accept submissions by theme and magazines that accept submissions about anything.

Themed Magazines

For some magazines, each individual issue has a different theme, and they expect each story submitted to involve that theme. For example, for the magazine *Conjunctions*, the theme for the Fall 2012 issue is Colloquy, meaning a conversation or public dialogue, and for your story to be accepted, it will have to involve a colloquy, even if it's just figurative.

Another example is the speculative fiction magazine, *Pedestal*, whose August 2012 issue requires submissions to be about the "Adventures of Mark Nipple," a fictional character who they bestow with various details. While your "Mark Nipple" story could still be quite imaginative, if you don't write about the theme, they won't accept your story.

You can find a calendar for the themes of hundreds of different literary magazines at duotrope.com.

General Magazines

Most magazines, however, have no theme restrictions, which is both easier and, in a way, more difficult. Magazines that are more prescriptive with their guidelines still have their own rules and criteria about what work they will publish. The rules are just left unsaid.

General magazines will still sometimes create a themed issue. However, they will always explain the theme on their website, and they will usually still accept general submissions.

Do It Right Now

Before you move on to the next section, subscribe to at least one literary magazine. Go to our resource on letswriteashortstory.com or the list of magazines in Appendix A and pick a magazine that looks interesting to you. You can't write short stories if you don't read short stories.

2

EFFECTIVE STORY WRITING STRATEGIES

Some people write stories where nothing much happens. The main character sits around thinking of things that happened in the past. The hero doesn't do anything heroic.

The only thing that matters in your story is what the characters do. What they think, feel, or see is just the whipped cream, peanuts, and cherry on top. The ice cream, the core of your story is what they do.

Sometimes people think that to write a realistic story, they can't have spectacle, intrigue, suffering, or excitement. I like what Robert McKee's character in the movie *Adaptation* says when a screenwriter tells him he's writing a movie where nothing much happens, just like life in the real world. McKee says:

Nothing happens in the world? Are you out of your f***ing mind? People are murdered every day. There's genocide, war, corruption. Every f***ing day, somewhere in the world, somebody sacrifices his life to save someone else. Every f***ing day, someone, somewhere takes a conscious decision to destroy someone else. People find love, people lose it. For Christ's sake, a child watches her mother beaten to death on the steps of a church. Someone goes hungry. Somebody else betrays his best friend for a woman. If you can't find that stuff in life, then you, my friend, don't know crap about life!

For your story to be realistic, something has to happen. You don't need to have explosions, murders, or dramatic love stories, but something has to happen.

Short Story Prompt

Write a scene where something happens, something involving murder, genocide, war, corruption, sacrifice, destruction, starvation, betrayal, or love.

Write About Death

If you're not sure what should happen in your story, write about a death.

Of the twenty best short stories in the 2011 Best American Short Stories, half of them involved a character dying.

Of the thirteen books nominated to the 2011 Booker Prize long list, every single one involved the theme of death.

Think about your favorite novels or films. How many of them involve a death?

If you want to give yourself a better shot not just at being published, but at writing a really good story, apparently you should write about death.

If you think about it, life and death are the only two themes shared by all of humanity, by every living thing since the beginning of time. Every person who has ever lived will die.

Death is the universal theme.

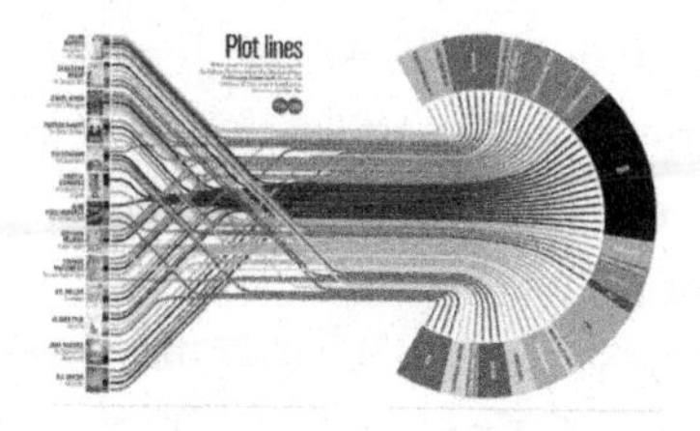

Above are the themes for the 2011 Booker Prize. See that big black part on the right? That's death.

We're fascinated by death. Two of the most popular books of 2011 were about what happens after you die. One was called *Love Wins*, a book questioning the existence of heaven and hell. The other was *Heaven is for Real*, about a boy who dies, goes to heaven, then is resuscitated and has uncanny knowledge about what heaven really looks like.

Thousands of stories are about how to avoid death, how to die well, how one person's death affected history, both personal and global. We love reading about death. Death is the great mystery of life, and mysteries have always belonged to the storytellers. So why not write about it? It might just be the thing that gets you published.

Short Story Prompt

Write a scene where a side-character, who the protagonist cares about, dies.

Three Effective Short Story Structures

There are two kinds of writers: One type loves structure and can't write without it. The other thinks structure is only for the uncreative and likes to write without it.

I'm not sure which is right. However, I do think every great writer uses some kind of structure, whether they know it or not. Flannery O'Connor, one of the most famous short story writers of all time, said she didn't tell her characters what to do; they told her. However, even her stories fall into traditional story structures that have always existed. If you can't stand structure, you don't have to use it, but you should at least know how good short story structures look.

Here are three structures that I've found incredibly helpful as I write short stories.

The Basic Three-Act Structure

The three-act story structure is found in films, novels, and yes, short stories.

In act one, the character discovers he has a problem.

In act two, he tries to solve the problem, failing again and again while slowly making everything worse. Eventually events escalate until he tries to solve his problem one last time. By the way, it's up to you as the storyteller to decide whether he succeeds or fails.

Finally, in act three, the character sits with his success or failure for a moment so we, the audience, know it's the resolution, the end of the story.

The Book Jacket Structure

The book jacket structure takes a theme, a phrase, a location, or an action from the beginning of the story and repeats it at the end, except with a twist. William Sydney Porter, an author who wrote under the pen name O. Henry (remember the PEN / O. Henry anthology we mentioned earlier?), used this strategy heavily, as Dr. John Yeoman notes. By echoing the beginning at the end, you give the story a sense of harmony and completeness.

A simple way to implement this strategy is to rewrite the beginning rather than the end. Rewriting the ending can sometimes be quite complicated. Instead, tweak the beginning by adding a motif, action, character, or, if you must, a whole scene.

I experimented with this technique on a story I had been writing on and off for two years. When I rewrote it using this technique, people who had read both versions told me the story was more powerful and had a better flow.

A Story With A Hole In It

In *Story Structure to Die For*, author and screenwriter PJ Reece says every good story is actually two stories. In the middle of the two stories, the character must have a transformative experience where he comes to the end of himself. In other words, he has to die, not physically, but metaphorically. The old person he used to be goes away, and a new person replaces him.

As you probably know, stories require the main character to change. If the character doesn't change, it's not a very good story. That's why Reece says there are actually two stories with a center point where the transformation takes place. One mistake that many writers make is that they end when they get to the transformation, the hole. They don't show how the protagonist has been changed by their "death." However, both stories are equally important, and if you just tell the first one up to the transformation you rob the reader of the resolution.

An Easy Trick to Save Time Writing Short Stories

In 2009, I was sitting in my friend's yard in Kenya, watching the chickens chase each other and drinking Kenyan *chai*—a strange, delicious tea that we found out later actually contains nicotine instead of caffeine. It was there that I made a decision:

It was time to write the novel I'd long been avoiding.

I only had a tiny netbook computer, which had screen about the size of my hand, but fueled by about ten cups of tea a day, I started writing my novel. One thousand words turned into five, five thousand words turned into ten.

Then, 15,000 words into the novel I got stuck, and everything fell apart. The novel had major structure flaws, the tea was giving me... digestive problems, and soon, I had to leave Kenya for Uganda, effectively ending my writing. Dozens of hours of work were wasted.

Or were they?

How to Recycle Novels Into Short Stories

Like me, you might have two or three half-finished novels abandoned on a computer hard drive somewhere. The good news is that all your hard work wasn't wasted.

Not only are your failed attempts at novel writing good

practice, they can also be recycled into short stories.

A few months ago, I was going through my archives when I saw that novel I started in Kenya. Most of it was worthless, but I realized one of the chapters would make a perfect short story.

How did I know? Here are three criteria to test whether you can recycle your novel into a short story:

1. Self-Contained

The chapter I chose was self-contained. In other words, it worked as a story even if separated from the rest of the novel.

While short stories don't always contain all the elements of plot, they should have a beginning and an end. You also want to find a segment that doesn't need too much backstory.

If it's not perfect though, just remember, you can always edit it.

2. Only One or Two Important Characters

Because short stories are so... well, short... you only have time to develop one or two major characters. That doesn't mean there won't be other characters in the story, but they take supporting roles, not the center stage.

3. A Transformative Moment

In every story, whether it's a short story, a novel, or a film, the character must have a transformative experience where she comes to the end of herself. The character must die, as PJ Reece puts it. Not physically, but rather she must transform in such a way that the person she used to be disappears, only to be replaced by a new, hopefully better, version of herself.

Look for those transformative moments in your half-finished novels. They just might make good short stories.

Short stories don't have to be written from scratch, and

by recycling them, you might be able to salvage them into something publishable.

Short Story Prompt

Go through your archives looking for stories to recycle.

To discover if it would make a good short story, follow these two steps:

1) What is it about, in one or two sentences?
2) Does it meet the three criteria above?

3

WRITE A BETTER STORY

Recently, I stayed up way too late reading Ben Marcus' short story, "What Have You Done," in the New Yorker. Short stories like this one are studies in brevity. You have a lot to do in just a few pages. And the first thing that gets cut is usually backstory.

How NOT to Begin Your Short Story

Backstory is defined simply as what happened before the story. Writers often use backstory to introduce you to new characters. You get to know where they live, what they do, their habits. I like to think of backstory as giving the reader a coffee date with your character.

However, backstory doesn't move the plot forward. It doesn't hold any conflict. Backstory easily becomes boring.

Here's why you should cut your backstory:

1. Cut backstory to add mystery.

Here's an example of how you should be introducing characters from Marcus' "What Have You Done." Notice how he first introduces one character named Andrea:

Even Andrea, at home, had to admit that Paul was not exactly handsome, per se, though when she was being affectionate she told him that he looked serious. He had a fair-minded face, she would say.

Question: Do you think Andrea is important to Paul and, potentially, to the plot of the story?

It sounds like it, right? It sounds like Andrea is his girlfriend or lover or wife. But all we get is clues, hints like "at home," or "when she was being affectionate."

The truth is Andrea is Paul's wife, but we don't find this out for two more pages, when she calls to check in on him. Since we don't know, it becomes a mystery. It makes us want to read on to find out who this Andrea person is.

2. Cut backstory to respect your reader's time and intelligence.

I once read a mystery novel where the first fifty pages were backstory. I quit reading. I didn't really care what the protagonist's apartment looked like or what she talked about with her neighbors.

I felt like the author had wasted my time.

Instead of spelling it out for us, throw us into your story. Don't introduce us into the world you've created. Don't tell us what everyone's favorite food is or what they like to do on a Saturday night. Let us figure it out on our own from the action of the story.

You must have conflict, and if your backstory has no conflict, save your readers' precious attention and chuck it.

3. Cut backstory because you just don't need it.

Some writers think you can't sympathize with a character until you get to know them intimately. However, the best way to introduce your characters to your reader is not through boring backstory. Instead, you introduce them by what they do. And if there's some detail from the past that you must explain to get a full sense of the character, an alternative to backstory is the flashback. A flashback shows a full scene from the past, whereas backstory just shares information.

In the end, it's the difference between showing and telling. Backstory is telling. Instead, introduce characters by showing what they do.

5 Elements of a Balanced Story

If you want to write a good (and publishable) short story, start by writing a balanced one. There are five elements of storytelling. These five elements are the building blocks of story, and if you focus on one element too much your story can get off-kilter and topple. The five elements are:

1. **Action.** What are your characters doing?

2. **Dialogue.** What are they saying?

3. **Description.** What are they seeing, hearing, touching, tasting, and smelling?

4. **Inner Monologue.** What are they thinking?

5. **Exposition / Narrative.** What other information does the narrator (i.e. you) want us to know?

Some people say there are more than five elements. I've

toyed with including emotion as another element, but that can be lumped into inner monologue. Other people add summary, but that can be considered exposition.

Every writer focuses on some of these elements more than others. Ernest Hemingway and Cormac McCarthy are heavy on the action, dialogue, and description side. Some of their novels give almost no inner monologue. Other writers like Charles Dickens and George Eliot use more narrative and inner monologue.

Let's look at some examples:

1. Action

Tommy drove to the park. He walked on the grass barefoot and looked up when he passed under the oak trees. After walking for a little while, he sat against one of the oaks, closed his eyes and fell asleep.

Notice all the action verbs: drove, walked, passed, walking, sat, closed, fell.

2. Dialogue

Tommy dreamt of his last conversation with Suzy.

"I'll never leave you," he said.

"You don't have to. I'll be gone in the morning."

"I'll follow you."

"You can. I'll just leave again, though."

"I'll follow forever if I have to."

"If you want to torture yourself, be my guest."

In dialogue, make sure you only use the verb said (as in he said / she said). You might be tempted to mix up your speaker tags with verbs like exclaimed, shouted, whispered, added, countered, and so on. However, readers tend to ignore speaker tags, and varying them is distracting and doesn't add to the dialogue. While it might feel more professional to you, it's actually the sign of an amateur. That being said, an occasional "he asked" is okay.

Also, many editors don't like it when authors use dialogue as the first line of their stories, instead preferring stories that set the scene and give the reader enough context to work out who's talking and to figure out what's going on. Take this advice for what it's worth. Some stories work better when they begin with dialogue. Just be aware of their concern and consider your story accordingly.

3. *Description*

Tommy woke to the feel of a warm breeze on his cheeks and bare arms. The oak leaves struck into each other in the wind and sounded like an audience of elves applauding. He smelled the grass and the breeze tasted like lemon and iron.

Description is a great way to pace your story. If you put a few sentences of description between your action and dialogue elements, your story won't move too quickly for the reader. Don't use too much description at one time though or your reader will get bored.

4. *Inner Monologue*

He thought of her and wondered where she was. He wondered if she was in trouble or with another man. He should follow her. He would get up in just a second. He just needed to sit there for a second more and breathe in the breeze and taste the air. Then he would go.

Inner monologue is the thing that sets apart writing from most other art forms. In film or theater, the audience rarely has access to the minds of the characters. Maybe that's why the interview cutaway has become so popular on shows and films like The Office, Modern Family, and *When Harry Met Sally*.

However, if you overuse inner monologue your story will sound young, like a diary or a young adult novel. It's also easy to lose the plot of the story if you use too much, and you can begin to tell too much and not show enough.

5. Exposition / Narrative

But he didn't go, and Tommy never saw Suzy again, though he thought of her often and with regret. He stayed in Texas and fell in love with other women, none of whom he married or even talked to much. He lived alone and died in the house they both lived in all those years ago.

Exposition is when the narrator takes over the story, often through some kind of summary or information dumping. It's like a voice over in a movie.

Exposition is necessary in almost all stories. However, it's an example of telling, and you want to show as much as possible. Use it sparingly.

Short Story Prompt

Write a story about Tommy using all the elements above. To practice, write the storytelling element you used after each sentence. Later, look over all your element tags and notice whether you lean toward one element or another.

8 Literary Techniques of Prize-Winning Stories

We all know there are stories and then there are "literary" stories. When you read Margaret Atwood, it just feels different than when you read Tom Clancy. And for some reason, it's literary writing that wins all the most prestigious awards like the Pulitzer Prize, the Man Booker Prize, and the Nobel Prize for Literature.

Literary authors are known for their unique voices and experimental styles. You might have learned not to write run-on sentences in school or to avoid beginning a sentence with "and," but literary writers often seem to flaunt their rule-breaking ways.

This is both good and bad. Literary stories can be difficult to understand, but they can also be beautiful to read, like poetry.

So if you're salivating to win a Nobel Prize, and just don't think your diplomacy skills are good enough to win the Peace Prize, here are eight techniques you can use to make your writing more "literary."

1. Write long sentences.

Long sentences can make for beautiful, complex prose that you want to read again and again to fully appreciate.

Hemingway and Faulkner, who both won the Nobel Prize in literature, along with James Joyce and all those other 1920s modernist authors, were known for their long, run-on sentences, full of conjunctions and lacking "correct" punctuation. Contemporary writers, like Cormac McCarthy, Ray Bradbury, and Tim O'Brien, do the same. Here's a quote from O'Brien's *The Things They Carried* illustrating it clearly:

Now and then, however, there were times of panic, when

they squealed or wanted to squeal but couldn't, when they twitched and made moaning sounds and covered their heads and said Dear Jesus and flopped around on the earth and fired their weapons blindly and cringed and sobbed and begged for the noise to stop and went wild and made stupid promises to themselves and to God and to their mothers and fathers, hoping not to die (18).

Isn't that beautiful?

2. *Write short sentences.*

Writing long sentences can exhaust your reader. If you follow up an extremely long sentence with a short snappy one, you can whip your reader to attention. Notice how Cormac McCarthy does it in *Suttree*:

One thing. I spoke with bitterness about my life and I said that I would take my own part against the slander of oblivion and against the monstrous facelessness of it and that I would stand a stone in the very void where all would read my name. Of that vanity I recant all (414).

Try reading it aloud. Notice how that last sentence feels like a gavel, cracking in a loud courtroom?

3. *Be lyrical.*

Literary writers are interested not just in what their words mean, but also in how they sound. The technical term for this is phonoaesthetics, the study of the sound of words and sentences. Like poets, literary writers want their words to melt on their reader's tongue like rich, dark chocolate. They want their readers to stop and say, "Mmm," and stare off into the distance contemplating all that is beautiful.

There are a few techniques writers use to make their

writing more euphonic, including alliteration, assonance, and consonance, but the best way to develop your "ear" for lyrical writing is to read other lyrical writers very slowly. You might pick up some Annie Dillard, William Faulkner, or Virginia Woolf.

We'll go over this more in the next section.

4. *Make an allusion to the Bible or* **Moby Dick** *or Milton.*

Literary writers are well read. They realize their writing doesn't exist in a vacuum, and so they subtly pay homage to the classic writers who have gone before them, which also deepens the meaning of their own work.

To make an allusion, you use an image, a character, or even a direct quote from another work of literature. These act as portals, coloring your story with the meanings wrapped up in the work you're referencing.

Also, it makes those who "get it" feel special, like they've been introduced into a secret world in the artist's mind.

Here's an example from the first page of Cormac McCarthy's *Blood Meridian*:

> His folk are known for hewers of wood and drawers of water but in truth his father has been a schoolmaster.

Did you get the allusion? Try reading it again.

Still didn't get it?

Ok, let's do a bit of detective work. If you google "hewers of wood and drawers of water," you'll find that it comes from the King James Bible. In Joshua 9, the Hivites deceived the Israelites into making a pact with them even though God told the Israelites to destroy them. When they found out they were deceived, the Israelites made the Hivites their slaves, people to chop wood and carry water.

What does that mean in Cormac McCarthy's novel? It means two things: the main character is deceptive and white trash.

But you might ask, *Who would possibly get that? It's so obscure!*

I would answer, *Exactly!*

The few people who figure the allusion out feel elite and sophisticated. Knowing something that other people don't is one of the most powerful feelings in the world. Like an inside joke, it creates a bond with your reader.

5. *Use an eponym to name your characters.*

Another way to use allusion is to name one of your characters after a character in another work. This technique works as a kind of literary pun, and creates an implicit association, a shared relationship, with the character in the other work.

6. *Be specific.*

Literary writers often study the vocabulary of the subject they're writing about. They want their writing to be precise. For example, if they're writing about nature, rather than just talking about the trees, they might describe the tulip poplar, the white oak, the eastern red cedar.

If they're writing about birds, they might avoid describing them as the red bird or the blue bird, but rather the kingfisher, the painted bunting (my personal favorite), or the yellow-bellied sapsucker.

7. Write a story within a story (or a story within a story within a story).

The story-within-a-story is one of the oldest literary techniques, and it's a simple way to create rich, multi-layered stories.

It works simply by having one of your characters tell another character a story, and this second story becomes the main story of the novel. Think *Arabian Nights*, where Scheherazade tells the Sultan story after story and eventually manages to make him fall in love with her.

Or Shakespeare's *Taming of the Shrew*, where the story of Petruchio "wedding and bedding" Katherina is set within another play about a drunk tricked into thinking he's rich.

Or Salman Rushdie's *Midnight's Children*, where the protagonist writes his memoirs as he narrates them to his mistress.

8. Have a wide scope.

Literary novels tend to have a wide, national or international scope, even if they portray local events. Hemingway, for example, often set his novels within the context of great wars, like World War I or the Spanish Civil War. Fitzgerald's *Great Gatsby* is considered a portrait of the "Lost Generation" and the Roaring 20s because of its memorable characters who were caught up in the decade's debauchery. Rushdie's *Midnight's Children* is about the rise and "fall" of India, from Independence to Indira Gandhi's injustices.

You may not want to win a Pulitzer, but if you do want to give your writing a touch of literary flair, these techniques are a good place to start. By far, the best way to learn more about these techniques, though, is to read more literary fiction. The examples I mentioned above are novels, but the techniques can be used in short stories as well. You might read the following:

For Whom the Bell Tolls by Ernest Hemingway
The Blind Assassin by Margaret Atwood
Blood Meridian by Cormac McCarthy
Midnight's Children by Salman Rushdie
A Portrait of the Artist as a Young Man by James Joyce
Absalom! Absalom! by William Faulkner

How to Make Your Story Sound Prettier

Some writers write prose that sounds good. The writing makes you want to read it slow, as if you could let the words melt on your tongue. I once read some of Faulkner's *Sartoris* out loud to a friend. Faulkner is known for his long, convoluted sentences and huge jumps in the narrative. My friend said, "Wow. That's an intense sentence. Do you even understand that?"

"Kind of," I said. "But it's beautiful." The thing is I didn't need to understand it. The way the words sounded was enough.

The study of the sounds of words and sentences is called phonoaesthetics. Thus, someone who studies the sounds of words would then be called a phonoaesthete (isn't that a fun word?). And when the words and sentences sound pleasant together, it's called euphony—as opposed to cacophony.

To review:

- **Phonoaesthetics** — the study of the sounds of words whether pleasant or unpleasant
- **Euphony** — Pleasant sounding words and sentences

- **Cacophony** — Unpleasant sounding words and sentences

The question, then, is how do we make our writing sound more interesting? Here are four suggestions:

1. *Alliteration*

Alliteration is the repetition of the first letter of the word throughout a sentence. Alliteration gives a sentence flow. If each letter were a color, it would be like painting with a palette of corresponding colors. Alliteration smoothes out hard edges and creates smooth lines. Here's a quick example.

Tommy took the truck to the train station.

Lots of repeated t's there. Below is an example from Herman Melville's *Moby Dick*. See if you can spot the alliteration:

Um-m. So he must. I do deem it now a most meaning thing, that that old Greek, Prometheus, who made men, they say, should have been a blacksmith, and animated them with fire.

Did you see it? Right, the m's throughout the sentence and a few d's in the beginning. Try reading it out loud. See how well the sentence flows. Melville used alliteration all over the place, and he is considered one of the great American masters.

2. *Consonance*

Consonance is the repetition of consonant sounds inside of a word. The repetition of consonants, especially hard consonants like t's and k's, tends to create cacophony rather than euphony. Here's another example from *Moby Dick*:

Ere the Pequod's weedy hull rolls side by side with the barnacled hulls of the leviathan...

Did you see it? I'll show the example again with the repeated consonants highlighted.

Ere the Pequod's weedy hull rolls side by side with the barnacled hulls of the leviathan...

Now do you hear all those "l" and "d" sounds? Read it again really slow and you'll see how the consonance ties the sentence together beautifully. The l's almost make you feel rolly, as if you are on the deck of a ship lilting in sea.

3. Assonance

Assonance is the repetition of vowel sounds inside of the word. Theoretically, assonance can create mood, even give you a light, airy feeling if you're repeating ae and ee sounds, or else a deep soulful feeling when repeating oe sounds. Finding assonance is a bit harder, but here's another example from *Moby Dick*:

And as though not a soul were nigh him...

Did you see it? I'll show it again with highlights.

And as though not a soul were nigh him...

Here, Melville repeats the ough sound, as in dough and mow. Theoretically, the emphasis of the ough sound should make you feel more expansive and soulful.

4. The Single BEST Way To Make Your Writing Sound Better

The best way to make your writing more euphonic is to read beautiful writing and read it slowly.

Here's why. Authors don't approach the blank page thinking, "Oh, I think I'll focus on assonance today. Hmm... maybe I should play with alliteration." No. They do it instinctively, and the best way to hone your instincts is through careful reading. When I was in college, my literature professor spent an entire day going through one paragraph of Faulkner's *Absalom! Absolom!* That one exercise taught me more about writing than the rest of the class.

Take a page or even just a paragraph of a piece of literature and read it slowly over five to ten minutes. Sound the words out as you go. Read aloud so that you can hear the words as well as visualize them. If you want to understand it even better, copy the passage out by hand.

Then, practice writing beautifully yourself.

Reading, more than anything else, will hone your instincts for phonoaesthetics.

Short Story Prompt

First, follow the link and pick a random passage of Moby Dick, *and read for at least five minutes. Choose just one or two paragraphs. Pay special attention to the sounds of Melville's prose. Let the rhythms sink into you. Then, just write. Write whatever story you're working on, and as you write, listen to the sounds and let your mind drift away. Focus on sound not meaning.*

A Secret Trick to Showing Rather than Telling

You've heard the classic writing rule, "Show. Don't Tell." It's one of the most common pieces of writing advice ever, and for good reason. Showing is really difficult.

Let me be clear, though, that it's impossible to fully eradicate telling from your style. Some telling is necessary or your short story would turn into an epic trilogy. The following is a simple trick I use to find the right balance.

Be more specific.

The simplest rule to remember if you're trying to show is just to be specific. Specificity will fill in the gaps from your telling and bring life to your scenes. Let me give you an example of how being specific will help you show.

Here's a very tell-y example:

> They went to New York to see *Cats*. They both enjoyed it very much. When they tried to go home, their flight was delayed because of the snow so they stayed another night and decided to see the musical again.

That's a fun story. A great trip to the city could be ruined by the weather, but they find a way to have fun. It's all pretty vague, though, isn't it? Who is they? Which theater did they see *Cats* at? Why did they enjoy it? How did they feel after their flight was delayed?

To show rather than tell, you have to interrogate your story and discover the specifics.

Here's that example with some of those questions answered:

> Tanya and James flew to New York City in a 747. They got their bags, took a taxi to their hotel, and checked into their rooms. "I can't wait to see the show. You're going to love it," said Tanya, but James shook his head. "I don't get it. It's about cats who sing and dance? Sounds sorta dumb." Tanya smiled, "Just trust me."
>
> Their hotel was just a few blocks from the Foxwoods Theater so they walked. He had never seen buildings so

> tall or so many people walking on the street. When they got to the theater, Tanya noticed his eyes were a little wider, his mouth a little slacker. The foyer was covered in gold and white marble, with hundreds of people milling around in gowns and beautiful suits. He didn't talk much. Finally, they took their seats, and the lights went down. He took her hand.

Let's stop there. Once you get specific your story can get a lot longer. This example is a little better, though. Instead of "they," we now see Tanya and James. We know a little more about them, that Tanya is a little more cultured, while James is more wary of it. We get a glimpse of the theater.

Interrogate Your Story

There's still more room for specificity, though, which is why you always have to interrogate your story.

What was their flight like? Why is James so awed by New York? What's the nature of their relationship?

Here's another example with some of those questions filled in with specificity:

> Tanya and James flew to New York in a 747. Tanya drank club soda and James had ginger ale. "Can I have the whole can?" he said to the blonde stewardess, whose lips tightened into a thin line, but she gave him the green can. When they landed at LaGuardia, James turned to her and said, "Just so you know, that was the first time I've ever flown anywhere."
>
> "What?" said Tanya. "Why didn't you tell me?"
>
> "I didn't want you to know I hadn't left Oklahoma."
>
> She took his hand and kissed it and held it to her cheek.
>
> "I'll still love you, even if you are an Okie hillbilly."

They both smiled and he kissed her.

That's definitely more specific, but it's also getting longer. We haven't even gotten to the theater yet.

I hope you see by now that every story is like an accordion. You can get infinitely more specific, but the consequence of specificity is length. While you should want to be more specific, to show more than you tell, you'll need to cut whatever fails to add to your story. The writer's job is to choose those specific details that are most important—usually during the editing stage—and cut all the rest. Be more specific, but don't bore us.

Short Story Prompt

Rewrite the following story by being more specific:

They went to Los Angeles to see his parents.

4

GET RID OF WRITER'S BLOCK

About a year ago, I spent four hours trying to figure out what to write. I had a deadline and had to publish something. I even had four or five good ideas. But I was stuck and couldn't get started.

I had writer's block.

As I thought about why I couldn't write, I realized I was blocked for three main reasons:

- Someone I respected had recently criticized my writing.
- Shortly after, I didn't get a writing job I really wanted.
- Shortly after that, a writing mentor of mine said a piece I had written for him as a favor "needed a lot of work."

Taken individually, none of these would have been that big of a deal, but together, they sent me down a shame spiral. "It's true. I'm a terrible writer," I thought. "I have no taste. I'm immature. Everyone can read my blog now and see how much I suck. Yada yada yada. Shame shame shame."

The Worst Sentence in the World

The hardest part of getting over writer's block is to realize you're blocked. Once you know you're sick, it's pretty easy to cure yourself.

You just have to allow yourself to write the worst sentence in the world.

Barry Michels[5] is a psychologist in Hollywood who charges screenwriters $375 an hour to fix their writer's block. He once told a screenwriter to kneel in front of his computer for one minute every day, praying to the universe for the ability to write the worst sentence in the world. The worst sentence in the world? Unsurprisingly, the screenwriter thought Michel's advice already was the worst sentence in the world. Still, for $375 an hour, he might as well try. For weeks, he knelt at his computer, feeling like a fool, and prayed for the ability to write the worst sentence in the world. A few months later he had written an Academy Award winning screenplay.

What happened? Why did seeking failure lead to success? How can writing the worst sentence in the world cure writer's block?

1. Because it frees you from perfectionism.

When I get blocked, it's because I'm trying to write the perfect blog post or the perfect short story or the perfect book. This is impossible and not worth the effort. Writing something open and vulnerable, on the other hand, is worth the effort.

If you give yourself the freedom to fail, you might actually succeed.

2. *Because you can't inspire yourself.*

In February of 2009, bestselling author Elizabeth Gilbert made a fascinating claim at the TED conference:

There is no such thing as genius.

Inspiration doesn't come from you. It is a gift from something outside of you, from the Muse, and if you write terribly, it's not wholly your fault. All you can do is show up, sit at your computer, and write.

Let go of the outcome of the future and allow yourself to live in the mess of the now.

3. *Because it's impossible.*

Writing the worst sentence in the world is just as impossible as writing the best sentence, but for some reason, when you intentionally aim to do something awful, terrible, simply no good, it frees you to do your best work.

If you give yourself permission to be a sucky writer, you allow yourself to be great.

Short Story Prompt

Whether you're blocked or not, try to write the worst sentence in the world. Spell things incorrectly and make grammatical errors. Write something you know is boring. Use all your style and technique to write a sentence that utterly fails.

Just Give Up

In the spring of 1965, Bob Dylan was finished. Dylan wanted nothing more to do with the music business. He had just finished an exhausting six-month tour. He never wanted to play any of the songs he had become famous for again—songs like "Blowing in the Wind" and "The Times They Are a Changing." In an interview with *Playboy* a year later, he said, "Last spring. I guess I was going to quit singing. I was very drained, and the way things were going, it was a very draggy situation." He told his manager he was buying a cabin in upstate New York, was quitting the music business, and was going to write novels.[6]

He was only there for a few days when he met what he called a "ghost," and an "uncontrollable urge" to write came over him. He basically word-vomited into his notebook. "It's like a ghost is writing a song like that," he told *Guitar World Acoustic* in 2004, "it gives you the song and it goes away. You don't know what it means. Except that the ghost picked me to write the song."

Four weeks later, he and his band were in the recording studio, and after four takes they recorded "Like a Rolling Stone," the song that would change Rock and Roll forever.

Personally, I can relate to Dylan's experience. Can't you?

When I wrote my first book, I was so frustrated at one point that I lay facedown on the floor moaning, thinking, "I don't want to write this book. I don't want to write anything. I don't want to be a writer anymore because I never want to feel this stupid again."

It sounds dramatic, but at some point on almost every writing project I've ever worked on, I came to a breaking point like this. It doesn't feel as much like writer's block as life block.

The truth is that the most important thing you can do for your creativity is to quit, to relax, to give up. Because if you relax better, you'll write better. Only three weeks after wanting to quit writing my first book, I had finished the final draft of the manuscript. I had a similar experience with a short story once, where I nearly gave up writing fiction altogether. Two days later the story was finished and shipped off to a few literary magazines.

With writing, as with every creative act, there is such a thing as trying too hard. You can strive when you need to do the opposite. Sometimes, we writers just needed to sit in our stories and play.

Today, relax.

Today, stop beating your head against the desk trying to finish your writing.

Today, sit in your story and play.

Today, give yourself permission to enjoy your writing.

Today, don't rush to finish, to meet your word count goal, to pound out stories. Instead, enjoy the process. Relax. Take a deep breath. Let your words be like the ocean, lapping the shores of a yellowsanded beach, the blue sky above.

Short Story Prompt

Free write. Don't think. Just write.

Is Your Story Worth It?

Finishing is the hardest thing for writers. It's also the most important. I used to have a difficult time finishing things. I would have a great idea for a novel or short story. I would get five or ten or twenty thousand words into it. And then I would get another new idea for a more interesting project and take off doing that. I have five or six unfinished novels on my computer hard drive. I call them my desert of bleached bones.

The famous novelist, Henry Miller, seemed to have the same issue. As he was laboring to finish his first novel, Tropic of Cancer, he wrote a set of eleven commandments and the first two dealt directly with his habit of flying off to every new project:

> 1. Work on one thing at a time until finished.
>
> 2. Start no more new books, add no more new material to "Black Spring."
>
> ...
>
> 10. Forget the books you want to write. Think only of the book you *are* writing.

You can see the rest of the list below.

Work Schedule, 1932–1933

–*Henry Miller Miscellanea*

COMMANDMENTS

1. Work on one thing at a time until finished.
2. Start no more new books, add no more new material to "Black Spring."
3. Don't be nervous. Work calmly, joyously, recklessly on whatever is in hand.
4. Work according to Program and not according to mood. Stop at the appointed time!
5. When you can't *create* you can *work*.
6. Cement a little every day, rather than add new fertilizers.
7. Keep human! See people, go places, drink if you feel like it.
8. Don't be a draught-horse! Work with pleasure only.
9. Discard the Program when you feel like it–but go back to it next day. *Concentrate. Narrow down. Exclude.*
10. Forget the books you want to write. Think only of the book you *are* writing.
11. Write first and always. Painting, music, friends, cinema, all these come afterwards.

Henry Miller's Commandments.

Why You Lack Discipline

We do this, don't we?

We dream up a new idea for a book, and since we are creative and emotional, we start working on that new project and abandon the one proving so difficult.

You get an idea, seemingly from God, and all you can see is possibility. It gives you chills; it makes your chest swell up with pride just to think about it.

How much better would it be to accomplish that novel, rather than waste away your time feeling like an idiot on the one you're working on? Wouldn't it feel so much better?

What Books Do You Want to Write Before You Die?

I empathize with this especially because for me, sometimes my gut feeling has been right. The novel I was working on wasn't very good. I have projects that I'm glad I abandoned. If I had finished them, they probably wouldn't have been published, and if they had been published, I wouldn't have wanted to put my name on them.

At the same time, if you don't finish something then what is the point of all this writing anyway? Someday, you will die, and all the stories you dreamed of writing will die with you. What do you have to complete to die satisfied?

By embracing your limits, you're able to prioritize the work that's most important. Rather than flying after any old idea that strikes you as interesting at the time, you start searching for just the few ideas you can devote your life to.

Is the story you're working on right now worth it? Why or why not? How can you change it to make it worth it?

5

EDITING TO PERFECTION

A few years ago, I wrote articles for the music section of a local weekly newspaper. Desperate for assignments, I agreed to an article with a brutal turnaround. The concert show my editor gave me to review would be over at one in the morning on Sunday night, and since the paper went to press on Monday, my article was due first thing Monday morning.

No bueno.

When I made it home at 1:30 AM after the show, I chugged a Coke and sat down at the computer. I spent most of the night writing, slept a few hours around three, and then got up to finish the rough draft before my day job at eight.

However, I had a problem. By the time I finished the article, I only had five minutes to edit 1,000 words. How was I going to do it?

Has this ever happened to you? Your English essay, newspaper article, book review, novel, or 900-page tome about the rise of democracy in Eastern Europe is due and you haven't finished editing it? Or maybe the submissions are closing for the writing contest you're submitting a short story to and you only have a few more minutes.

How to Edit When You Don't Have Time to Edit

You can make these three edits in five minutes or less, and your teacher/editor/publisher will be smiling when they read it. Well, maybe not smiling, but at least they won't be crying and shredding your manuscript up into bits. You could also take an hour, and work on these same edits and have a much better story.

Step One: Replace Weak Verbs.

Search (CTRL + F for Windows or CMND + F) for weak verbs like the following:

- is
- was
- am
- were
- being
- are
- get
- got

Replace these "weak-sauce" verbs with something stronger. For example, don't write, "Spot *was running* through the woods." Instead, "Spot *ran* through the woods." Not "She *got* them a present." Instead, "She *gave* them a present."

2. *Remove Adverbs.*

Search (CTRL + F) for "ly" and take out adverbs, replacing with concrete detail.

Adverbs tend to tell more than they show, and instead of saying, "He laughed heartily," write something like, "He slapped the table as his laugh shook the room."

3. *Take out other weak words.*

Start by searching (CTRL + F) for "that." Cut as many as you can without ruining the structure.

Not "The dress that she wore tore at the seam." Instead, "The dress she wore tore at the seam."

A few more cuttable words:

- very
- really
- thing
- stuff
- almost
- I think
- Much
- just
- so
- people

I think this stuff is very easy, almost the easiest thing you could really do. (See what I did there?)

Stop Using the Word "Some"

If you're using the word "some" in your creative writing, you're not being specific enough.

For example, here is a sentence with the word "some":

Tom liked to play guitar but didn't take it as seriously as some.

Who is some? Why do they take it so seriously, and how does Tom know he doesn't take it as seriously as they do? Does Tom really like playing the guitar or does he just put up with it?

This sentence leaves more questions unanswered than it answers. By replacing the word "some" with a more specific phrase, we can do a better job characterizing Tom:

Tom liked to play guitar but didn't take it as seriously as his brother Jim, who sometimes came downstairs with bloody band-aids on the tips of his fingers after playing for hours.

See how much better that is? We get a clearer picture of Tom and how he feels about the guitar. However, it's still not perfect. There's still a form of "some." Instead of being vague about who, I was vague about when. Here's an ultra-specific rewrite without "sometimes":

Tom liked to play guitar but didn't take it as seriously as his brother Jim. Jim got his first guitar for Christmas when he was fourteen. Tom was eleven, and he remembered how Jim came downstairs the next morning, his fingers all wrapped in bloody band-aids, the wince on his face as he picked up his spoon.

By placing our example in a specific time, we get a clearer picture of both Jim and Tom. Now we know why Tom doesn't take it as seriously as "some." We can make an educated guess that he probably enjoys playing, that he admires his brother, but isn't passionate about it enough to experience the pain he watched his brother go through.

If you want to bring life to your characters, stop using the word "some." Instead, look at it as a chance to fill in the blanks in your story and in your characters.

Before you submit your work in progress, make it better by getting rid of the word "some." Press CTRL + F (or Command + F in OSX) and search for "some." For each instance, see if you can rewrite "some" to be more specific. You can do this for some, sometimes, something, somewhere, and someday, too.

Get Peer Feedback

The best advice I can give you about editing is to stop editing. It's possible to go over your story so many times that you will start to do more harm than good. You can get so close to your work that you no longer become objective, and at that point, you need a reader with fresh eyes. That's why as soon as I can, I send my short stories to a group of other writers and readers I respect. After getting their feedback, I have a much better idea of what my story actually is rather than what I think it is or would like it to be.

However, not everyone has a network of writing friends they can send their stories to. Here's a list of five ways to get people to look at your work.

1. Join a critique group.

Many cities have groups of writers who meet regularly to critique each other's work. You can often find critique groups at meetup.com. If your city doesn't have a writer's group, start one of your own![7]

2. *Use social media.*

Twitter, Facebook, Instagram, and LinkedIn are all great places to meet other writers who could potentially be critique partners. You can join writing groups on LinkedIn, participate in the conversation on Facebook pages for writers (start with The Write Practice's page!), and go on Twitter and search for "authors" and "writers."

Before you ask other authors to look at your work, make sure you develop a relationship with your new friends over several weeks. No one appreciates someone who asks for a favor right away.

Another way to use social media to easily find critique partners, share a tweet or Facebook status update like the following:

"Whew... I just finished my latest short story! I'm looking for a few amazing people who will read it and give me feedback. Help a writer out?"

When I do this, I'm always amazed and grateful at how many people are willing to read my work.

3. *Read (or write) writer's blogs.*

I started The Write Practice in part because I didn't have a community of writing friends and I wanted to create one. And it worked.

Everyday, writers give each other feedback and help each other in the comments section. Several of these commenters have become real life friends. I've learned that being active in the comments of writer's blogs is a great way to find writers you respect.

If you want to find a community of writers who can read and critique your short stories, find a few writing blogs and start participating in the discussion.[8] If you're feeling more ambitious, you can even start your own.

4. Join a short story class.

The knowledge you get from writing classes is good, but the people you meet are even more important. Writing classes are great places to build community with other writers who can help you.

You can find classes through your local university or community college, or you can find an online class through Writer's Digest or Gotham's Writing Workshop.

If you like this book, we have a writing community focused specifically on short stories at thewritepractice.com. Swing by the site to find out more.

6

SUBMITTING YOUR SHORT STORY

After you finish your story, you come to the real challenge: submitting it.

Recently, I sent a story off, and afterwards, I wrote on Facebook, "Just submitted a short story to 4 literary magazines. Yuck. It kind of feels like dropping off your baby at a day care with thousands of other crying babies, run by underpaid workers who hate you."

We run a short story contest through The Write Practice and afterwards, I always hear how hard it was for people to submit their stories. "Submitting is like sitting naked in the subway," said one reader. Another said, "I've never submitted anything. And after I hit submit, I wanted to hide under my blankets. I still do."

Submitting is hard.

"Real Artists Ship."

The unfortunate truth is that if you don't submit you won't improve as a writer. You'll grow stagnant and bored and eventually you will give it up completely.

I like what my friend Brian said after my dramatic Facebook comment, “Don’t be a helicopter parent. Let your child grow up. If you did your job as a parent it will be just fine.” Like all parents learn when they drop their kid off at daycare for the first time, you have to let go.

This is how you become a real writer. You submit. You submit your short stories and your essays and your novels. You face the possibility (probability, really) of rejection. You submit because your job as a writer is to write things for others. If you just write for yourself, you are not a writer. You are a journaler.

Which is fine, if that’s what you want to be.

However, as Steve Jobs said, “Real artists ship.”

An award-winning author I have an acquaintance with told me all you can do is write the best story you can. If your story isn’t picked, “persevere.”

The only thing you can do is to submit your story, send it to the world, and then get started on the next one.

Submission Shopping List

Before we begin talking about how to submit your manuscript, you need to get a few supplies. If you don’t already have them, run to your office supply store and to the post office to pick up the following:

- Letter size envelopes (#10)
- 9x12 size envelopes
- Stamps

If you want extra credit, pick up a box of printable mailing labels as well. These are optional, but printed labels look more professional than handwritten ones, especially if your handwriting is as bad as mine. Also, if you don't already have one, you'll need a printer and some paper.

Some magazines still don't take online submissions. You'll need these supplies to get your manuscript to them. You'll send your manuscript in the 9x12 envelope with a self-addressed, stamped envelope (SASE) so they can reply to let you know they accepted (yay!) or rejected (shoot!) your story.

Most manuscripts weigh between three and four ounces. So if you hate going to the post office more than necessary, you can buy stamps in advance that add up to the price of postage. As of July 2012, a three ounce, large envelope costs $1.30 in postage and a four ounce $1.50. You can find an updated price list on the USPS website.[9]

One Easy Mistake That Could Get You Instantly Rejected

Literary magazines expect you to submit your story in a very specific format, and if you don't follow this format, they may reject your piece without even reading it. This is why it's so important to read the submission guidelines of every publication before you send them your work. You can find this information on their website, and if you check the list of publications in Appendix A, you'll find links directly to their guidelines.

However, while each publication will tell you how to format your manuscript specifically for them, they probably won't tell you the standard formatting that most publications expect.

If you want your story to be published, you'll have to learn standard formatting. Imagine reading hundreds of stories every month and then getting that one odd story written in Comic Sans or some cursive font. You want your story to stick out but not like that!

If you have a writing program like Scrivener[10] it will automatically put your manuscript in the correct format for magazines. But if you're just using Microsoft Word or a similar program, you'll have to format it yourself.

In this section, I'll show you how to format your manuscript so the editors will at least give your story a chance and not throw it out at first glance.

On the next page, you can see the standard format for short stories. At the top you write your name and address. On the opposite side, include the word count rounded to the nearest 100.

Your title should begin 1/2 to 2/3 of the way down the page.

Always double space.

The standard font is Courier. While some publications accept Arial or Times New Roman, I would play it safe and go with Courier unless the Submission Guidelines say otherwise. Margins should be one inch on all sides.

Use tabs to show paragraphs, like in a book, rather than line spaces, like on a blog.

U.R. Name
1234 I Live Here Road
Springfield, IL 10001
555-555-5555
youremail@gmail.com

Word count
rounded to nearest 100
ex: 3,400 words

YOUR TITLE CAPITALIZED

by U.R. Name

As you can see, this is the standard formatting for short stories. At the top you write your name and address. On the opposite side, include the word count rounded to the nearest 100.

Your title should begin 1/2 to 2/3 of the way down the page.

Always double space.

The standard font is Courier. While some publications accept Arial or Times New Roman, I would play it safe and go with Courier unless the Submission Guidelines say otherwise. Margins are one inch on all sides.

Use tabs to show paragraphs, like in a book, rather than line spaces, like a blog.

Name / Title / 2

At the top of every page except for the first, include a header with your last name, a shortened version of your title (no more than three words), and the page number. You will never staple your manuscript, so including a header is essential so the editor doesn't lose pages of your manuscript.

That's how you format your short story. Not too difficult, right?

At the top of every page except for the first, include a header with your last name, a shortened version of your title (no more than three words), and the page number.

Never staple your manuscript. Editors like the pages loose, usually even free of a paperclip. This means that including a header is essential so the editor doesn't lose pages of your manuscript.

If you need to print out a cheat sheet, you can find the Short Story Formatting Checklist in Appendix B.

What is a Cover Letter and Are They Necessary?

The cover letter for your short story is similar to the cover letter you include with your resume. Here are the components:

- **The Address.** "Dear Fiction Editor," will suffice, but see if you can find their name on the magazine's website.
- **The Title of Your Manuscript.** The first line mainly shares the title of your manuscript. It's traditional to include a word-count, but that isn't terribly important since the word-count should be included on the first page of your manuscript.
- **Bio.** Your bio shouldn't be more than thirty words long, and should contain your writing credits, if you have any.
- **Simultaneous Submission?** If you're submitting your story simultaneously to other magazines as well, mention that. However you don't have to say where you're submitting to.
- **Signoff.** Thank them again, write your name, and that's all!

Most magazines expect cover letters, but they'll often be the first to tell you they're not that important. For example, Duotrope asked editors[11] from top magazines on the subject of the cover letter, and here are a few things they said:

"Cover letters and previous publications do not matter for us at *Caketrain*, but we do like to have contact information so that we can reach the submitter." Amanda Raczkowski, *Caketrain*

"I don't have much time available for reading cover letters. No information is fine. A few words about previous publications are okay, but won't sell the story. I run a bit of biographical information with each story, but I always ask for that information after I purchase the story. There's no need to worry about including it in the cover letter." Sheila Williams, Asimov's *Science Fiction*

"[We want to know] whatever they want to reveal, in a paragraph or less. Other publishing credits might be of interest but are not necessary. Plot summaries or topics covered in poems are absolutely NOT needed, and generally hurt. A good cover letter can focus our attention on the submission, but a bad one can prejudice us against the work, so it is really a 50-50 situation. It's fine to submit without cover letter." Wendy Lesser, *The Threepenny Review*

"We love cover letters and learning interesting details about the writers who send their work to PANK. That said, we don't need a cover letter to consider your work and we're not impressed by a long list of your credentials." Roxane Gay, *PANK*

"We don't care at all about cover letters. It's nice to at least drop us a 'hello' or a 'thank you' or an 'I like your magazine' (but be sure to make it sound sincere). We never read bios before responding to a submission. We like the submission to do the talking, not the past of the author." Nathaniel Tower, *Bartleby Snopes*

"We love succinct bios that convey a writer's experience —whether or not it includes publishing experience. Lists of publication credits do matter, but not as much as the quality of the writing. We have published several writers who had never been published before. That's rare, but we're open to it." Jeff McMahon, *Contrary*

"We're happy to have authors skip the cover letter. If they

do list previous publication credits, we may or may not glance at them. Telling us what we're supposed to get out of your story is unlikely to help you in any way." Jonathan Laden, *Daily Science Fiction*

"Actually, we don't need to know anything about the person. Submishmash has a section for 'comments,' but we don't require biographical information or a list of previous publications. The work should speak for itself." Beth Staples, *Hayden's Ferry Review*

I hope that removes all misinformation or fear you had about the cover letter. The best cover letter in world won't help you get published. Don't waste more than a few minutes on it. Instead, work on your story.

If the magazine requests email submissions, the body of your email can suffice as a cover letter. If the magazine uses an online submission service like Submittable, there is usually a section of the form for cover letters. And if you're submitting through the mail, your cover letter is placed atop the first page of your manuscript.

Here's a sample cover letter:

Dear Fiction Editor,

Thank you for reading my enclosed short story, "A Rose for Emily."

I am from Oxford, Mississippi. While I was never able to make it in New York, and despite my constant struggle with alcoholism, I've managed to win a Nobel Prize and Two Pulitzers. If you don't publish me, you're an idiot.

I am submitting this story simultaneously.

Thank you for your time,

William Faulkner

Well, maybe don't follow that exactly, but you get the idea.

A Controversial Note About Simultaneous Submissions

As you read the guidelines of different literary magazines, you might find a magazine that doesn't accept simultaneous submissions. Simultaneous submissions is a term for sending your story to multiple magazines at once. If a magazine doesn't accept simultaneous submissions, you have to wait, sometimes up to six months, to hear back from them before you send it elsewhere.

However, while this may earn me the ire of a few editors, I recommend that you ignore this rule. Most major authors do.[12] This policy isn't fair to writers. If you had to do this for every publication, you could have to wait years before your piece was published.

Of course, if the publication does not accept simultaneous submissions, you will not want to mention you are submitting simultaneously in your cover letter.

7

HOW TO GET THE MOST OUT OF YOUR STORIES

In the online age, platforms have become key for success. Authors everywhere are being told they can't be published without a platform. Here's the formula:

1. Start a blog.
2. Post at least three times a week to build up traffic.
3. Guest post on other blogs to build a subscriber list.
4. Write an eBook. Give it away for free to subscribers to build your list further.
5. Keep doing this until you hit 1,000 subscribers.
6. Ding! You (might) have enough for a book deal.

However, this advice hasn't done much for fiction authors. Most fiction authors who have tried to build their platform end up blogging about writing. There are thousands of blogs about writing that don't have many followers. On top of that, people who read non-fiction don't always read fiction, so even if you do get a following, you might have trouble converting them into readers of your fiction.

Short Stories as a Platform

Your short stories, on the other hand, could be an effective addition to your platform strategy. For example, I spoke with Earl Wynn, the editor of the online literary magazine *Daily Love Stories* among others, who said some of his stories receive "between half and a quarter of a million views in a matter of weeks." While publishing short stories isn't the only thing you can do to build your platform, it is a great way to add authority and focus on fiction.

The Old Platform

This isn't a new idea. The main way fiction authors built their platforms in the past was by writing short stories for literary magazines. Years ago, all the big magazines, from *Cosmopolitan* to *Playboy*, carried short stories, and writers from Ernest Hemingway to Stephen King first got their start by publishing in magazines. However, for reasons we won't go into here, short stories went out of favor, and the magazines that do carry them have much smaller reader bases.

While short stories are still important for establishing your reputation among editors, agents, and publishers, they have become increasingly irrelevant as a way to build a platform and connect with real readers.

However, how else are you going to create a platform online? You can write a non-fiction blog and hope your audience likes your novel when you publish it. You can write a novel and sell it for $0.99, hoping the amount you sell will make up for the price. You can even give your novel away for free so that people will at least remember your name.

For writers who aren't interested in that and are looking

for another option, I believe short stories could be the answer. In fact, I think short stories could soon become the best platform builder for writers once again.

How to Create the New Short Story Platform

Platforms are about creating authority and connection with fans, and the strategy I'm about to suggest does both. It also relies on the fact that after literary magazines publish your story, the publishing rights revert back to you, either immediately or after a set time period (check the magazine's guidelines). This means that once they publish it, you can re-publish it as many times as you want, only it has now been "approved" by an authoritative literary magazine.

Here's the process broken down into five easy steps:

Step One: Build a website.

You can get a free website through Tumblr, Wordpress, or Blogger, but to look professional, I highly recommend getting a self-hosted Wordpress blog.[13]

Step Two: Install a newsletter signup form to your website.

Rather than creating a normal blog that you have to constantly update, all you really need is a blank page with a sign up form for people to receive your newsletter. An example I like is Brian Clark's entreproducer.com.

If you're looking for a good newsletter service, I recommend Aweber or Mailchimp.[14] Aweber is slightly more expensive, but it's a better service.

Step Three: Publish Short Stories!

Write short stories and get them published in the best magazines you can. The quality of magazines is important but quantity is even more important. You'll see why in the next step.

Step Four: When Your Story is Accepted . . .

Include a link to your new website in your author bio. When people read your story, they will go to your website and sign up for your newsletter. That way, you won't just be relying on them to remember your name. You'll be able to create a relationship with them.

Don't forget, when your story is published you need to share it with all your social media networks, including Facebook, Twitter, and your blog. Wynn says about the stories published on Daily Love Stories, "More than anything, I find that a story's popularity depends on how widely its writer is willing to advertise it. Those who do little or no promotional work rarely get beyond a hundred or so hits in a day." Even though it's not your platform, you're in charge of making your story successful.

Step Five: The Best Part

After the magazine publishes the short story, the publishing rights for the story revert back to you. Sometimes this happens immediately. Sometimes it takes ninety days. Again, it's important to read the submission guidelines and your contract.

Once they revert back to you, you can then self-publish your story and sell it through your website. Get someone to reformat your manuscript into the Kindle, Nook, or iPad format so you can upload it onto Amazon, Barnes & Noble, and the other online bookstores (if you don't know anyone who can convert your story, email me at joebunting@thewritepractice.com and I'll refer someone). I recommend pricing it between 99¢ to $2.99.

Your readers will be more likely to buy the story because it's been vetted and certified by a legitimate literary magazine, and this way, you can potentially make money on it twice. More importantly, it gives the people who subscribe to your newsletter more chances to read your work.

For those of you familiar with blogging, this strategy is like guest posting for fiction authors. And it's far better than writing a traditional blog because you don't have to waste your time writing non-fiction—and developing a non-fiction reading audience—when you'd rather be writing fiction.

CONCLUSION: WHAT THIS WRITING THING IS ALL ABOUT

It's safe to say there are more writers now than at any other time in history. I went to a writers' conference in Chicago in 2012, and there were 10,000 other writers there. The amount of creative writing programs at universities have exploded from about fifty in the 1980s to over 300 just in the US. There are over 110 million blogs.

At the same time, the publishing industry is going through a crisis. This crisis began in the music industry. The Internet destabilized the despotic grasp record companies held on the business. Then blogging and Craigslist combined to displace thousands of jobs in journalism. Now, the conflict has spread to publishing. Some icons like Seth Godin are saying writers might not deserve to get paid anymore:

Who said you have a right to cash money from writing? I gave hundreds of speeches before I got paid to write one. I've written more than 4000 blog posts for free.

Poets don't get paid (often), but there's no poetry shortage. The future is going to be filled with amateurs, and the truly talented and persistent will make a great living. But the days of journeyman writers who make a good living by the word–over.

Why do you write?

Do you write to make money? Do you write to get famous? Do you think you might become the next John Locke or Amanda Hocking or Stephen King or James Patterson?

It's possible. I won't lie. It could happen. And I do think you should be paid for your work. I hope you make lots and lots of money. Don't think I'm rooting against you.

The odds, though, are not in your favor. Below are four reasons that we write beyond making money, and I believe all our minor reasons for writing filter down into these four categories.

1. We write to be fully alive.

Sir Ken Robinson says:

The arts especially address the idea of aesthetic experience. An aesthetic experience is one in which your senses are operating at their peak; when you're present in the current moment; when you're resonating with the excitement of this thing that you're experiencing; when you are fully alive.

We write to be fully alive. Writing draws us into the moment. We see the blades of grass, hear the minuscule chirp of the morning cricket, watch the shade travel from one edge of the yard to the other, seemingly for the first time.

Writing helps us make art out of everyday, ordinary moments.

2. We write to make a name for ourselves.

George Orwell says one motivation to write is sheer egoism, that you write out of the "desire to seem clever, to be talked about, to be remembered after death, to get your own back on the grown-ups who snubbed you in childhood, etc., etc."

That's part of it, but I think the motivation goes much deeper than being well liked in the present moment.

If you're being honest, you would agree that it would be nice to live forever. But if you can't live forever physically, then why can't your memory live forever? We're still talking about Geoffrey Chaucer, Virginia Woolf, Mark Twain, and George Eliot long after their deaths. Why not you? While this might not be the most unselfish of motivations, it's certainly natural.

We write so our words, our memories, our very lives outlive the hand that wrote them.

3. We write to change the world.

People consume more than ever in the history of the world. We eat more, we listen to more music, and we consume more information. At the same time, we've learned enough about consumerism to know it won't make us happy.

Writing gives us a chance to turn the tides on consumerism. Rather than consume more, we can *make* something. Isn't that exciting? Every day, when you put your fingers to the keys, you're creating something. And then, with the click of a button, you can share it with the world. Humans have a built in need to make our mark on the world. We want to bring new things to life, to mold things into the image we have in our imaginations, to subdue the earth.

We write not just to change the world, but to create a new world.

4. We write to discover meaning.

The psychiatrist Victor Frankl said that the main search of mankind is not happiness or pleasure but meaning. "Life is never made unbearable by circumstances, but only by lack of meaning and purpose," he wrote in *Man's Search for Meaning*.

Writers are uniquely gifted to find meaning for themselves and to help others find meaning. In fact, this has always been the main task of storytellers. Every story matters to the person living it, and our job is to tell the universal stories, the stories that reveal the story of every person on the earth.

We write to bring meaning to the world.

The Real Reason to Write

We write short stories, we submit them, we publish in magazines or on our own, we do all this writing because art is worth creating. Even if we're not widely read, does it mean it's all in vain?

What if we decided it was enough to transform the life of one reader? Would that be worth it? What if that one reader is you? Writing can change your life. It can bring you alive. Why would you throw it away just because you might not make any money?

I write because I know I'm meant to. I know that I need to. It's good for my soul. It connects me to the human race. It keeps me alive.

Writers Bring Meaning to Pain

"In some ways suffering ceases to be suffering at the moment it finds a meaning, such as the meaning of a sacrifice," said Victor Frankl.

Every story requires pain and suffering. If the protagonist doesn't experience pain, he or she won't change. "Pain develops character. If you have a story where someone learns through joy, the audience won't buy it," said Donald Miller.

Joy is great. Your story should incorporate some joy. But pain is the Great Teacher.

Stop Submitting

You need to submit your work. Even if you don't think your short stories are good enough for *The New Yorker*, submit your work somewhere, even if you just post it on your blog. You will not grow as a writer unless you submit your work. If you learn nothing else from this book, I hope you learn that.

However, there is a danger to submitting your writing. When you submit your writing you become vulnerable. You risk failure. It can bring anxiety and shame. And it's possible, if you submit too much, to become cynical. It's possible to burnout on writing altogether. How do you write in such a way that you don't exhaust your creativity, smother the flame of inspiration, and allow writing to become merely another chore rather than a gift?

Six days a week, I write. I submit stories to literary magazines. I write as well as I can. One day a week, though, I stop writing. I stop submitting. I stop worrying about getting published altogether. Instead, I submit to rest. I spend time with my family. I eat and drink and enjoy the life I have been given.

Rest Brings Color to the World

I lived in California for over twenty-four years, and every day was basically the same: perfect. The spring / summer average temperature was seventy degrees. The fall / winter average was sixty. We only had to wear coats when we went snowboarding four hours away. We only got hot when we worked out.

It was perfect.

In 2010, I moved to Georgia, and saw my first fall. The whole world turned red and orange and brown and I had seen nothing like it before.

Soon, fall turned to winter. Coats and gloves and furry hats. It was a white Christmas.

Soon, winter turned to spring. One day it was winter and the next day, I walked outside and the cold didn't bite my cheeks and earlobes. I took off my coat.

Soon, spring turned to summer. Four months of ninety-five degree days. I kept my head down. I drank lots of water. I tried not to complain. One day, I came outside and the pressure was gone. A strong breeze came up on my back. I put on a sweater.

It was fall again. I had been there a year.

In California, every day was the same, but in Georgia, every day is different. The truth is, I prefer seasons. Winter makes spring better. Summer makes fall better. I need change, and a little suffering, to value anything for the gift it is.

Six days a week, I write so that I can submit stories and

get them published. I submit because I'm a writer, and because writers write for others.

One day a week, though, I stop submitting. I stop worrying about getting published altogether.

Instead, I submit to rest. I don't write. Or if I do, I don't do it for others. I do it for myself and for the sake of my soul. It's a break, a winter, a kind of Sabbath.

We rest so our work can be turned into something like prayer and not toil. Without days of rest and days of work, everything turns to gray.

As Rabbi Abraham Joshua Heschel says:

How else express glory in the presence of eternity, if not by the silence of abstaining from noisy acts? He who wants to enter the holiness of the day must first lay down the profanity of clattering commerce, of being yoked to toil. He must go away from the screech of dissonant days, from the nervousness and fury of acquisitiveness and the betrayal in embezzling his own life. He must say farewell to manual work and learn to understand that the world has already been created and will survive without the help of man. The world has our hands, but our soul belongs to Someone Else.

You rest because if you write for others for years and years it becomes a performance. You stop making art. You stop caring about craft. You get exhausted and resentful, angry at the thing that once gave you so much joy.

You rest to restore the relationship between your art and yourself, your hands and your heart, your work and your life.

You rest so you can submit again tomorrow.

LET'S WRITE A SHORT STORY

If you've come this far, thank you for reading. I hope you're inspired to get writing.

You might be wondering what's next, how are you going to apply all this newfound knowledge. As important as learning is, it's even more important to take action, and I hope this book provided you with the carrot on a stick (and the butt kicking) you needed to get started writing short stories.

However, you can't do it alone. All the best writers have had communities of other writers who supported them. If you're looking for help getting started or if you're already on your way and are looking for an opportunity to get stronger or give back, join us at Let's Write a Short Story.

This will be both a class and a community, giving you the opportunity to learn with a group of passionate writers who want to support you.

And by the end, I guarantee you will have written and submitted a short story or you get your money back (not without a lot of butt kicking though). Check it out at letswriteashortstory.com.

May you be inspired. May you be productive. May you be at peace.

Joe Bunting

LITERARY MAGAZINES TO GET PUBLISH IN

Have you ever wanted to publish a short story in a literary magazine but didn't know where to start. According to Duotrope.com, there are over 4,800 literary magazines today. Which ones are the best? How do you find the right for your story?

Below, I have handpicked 45 literary magazines that are among the best in their respective genres. While this isn't a complete list of all 4,800 literary magazines, it is a good place to get started with your research.

If the magazines below don't fit your particular writing style, check out duotrope.com. It's a fantastic search engine and aggregator of literary magazines. I find their 100 most favorited markets list particularly helpful (make sure to change the dropdown menu to "Most Favorited Markets").

If you write science fiction, fantasy, horror, or crime, you can find new anthologies and open submission announcements at Horror Tree.

For a complete explanation of how to research and submit to literary magazines, check out the book *Let's Write a Short Story!*

Have fun exploring all these literary magazines!

And for help on submitting your short stories for publication, check out this guide on how to publish a short story.

Note: This list changes frequently as new magazines are added and others close. Please check back frequently.

"Literary" Literary Magazines

Tin House
Crazy Horse
AGNI
Black Warrior Review
One Story
The New Yorker
The Threepenny Review
Zoetrope: All-Story
Boulevard
The Sun Magazine
McSweeney's Quarterly
Camera Obscura
Virginia Quarterly
The Atlantic
Granta
Pank

Science Fiction / Fantasy Literary Magazines

Strange Horizons
Clarkesworld
Fantasy & Science Fiction Magazine
Apex Magazine

Asimov's Science Fiction
Daily Science Fiction
Lightspeed
Beneath Ceaseless Skies
Andromeda Spaceway Inflight Magazine
Abyss and Apex
Analog Science Fiction and Fact
Psuedopod (audio stories!)

Horror Literary Magazines

Horror Tree
Unnerving
LampLight
Nightmare
The Horror Zine
Liminal

Flash Fiction Magazines*

Short Fiction Break (up to 2,000 words)
Horror Tree (100 words or less)
Daily Science Fiction
Vestal Review
Flash Fiction Online
Smokelong Quarterly
Foundling Review (up to 2000 words)
Every Day Fiction
Twenty20 (20 words or less)
Brevity (750 words or less)

**Flash Fiction is generally defined as 1,000 words or less, although some magazines allow stories as long as 1,500 words while others only accept stories under 500.*

SHORT STORY FORMATTING CHECKLIST

- Name, address, phone number, email in top left corner
- Word count in top right corner
- 12 point, courier font
- Double-spaced
- 1-inch margins
- Title and author name ½ of the way down first page
- Indented paragraphs, not line breaks
- Header with last name, abbreviated story title, and page # in top right corner beginning on page 2
- Pound sign (#) separating line breaks

Submission Package

- Unstapled, loose leaf

- Cover letter
- Self-addressed, stamped envelope (if submitting by mail)

AN ONLINE WRITING COMMUNITY TO HELP YOU BECOME A PUBLISHED WRITER

ENDNOTES

1 See "The Role of Deliberate Practice in the Acquisition of Expert Performance" by Ericsson, Krampe, and Tesch-Romer (1993): "We claim that deliberate practice requires effort and is not inherently enjoyable. Individuals are motivated to practice because practice improves performance." http://www.definingsomeday.com/wp-content/uploads/2010/05/EricssonDeliberatePracticePR93.pdf

2 *ibid.* "In support of this claim, he reported several laboratory studies and a study of experienced typesetters by Aschaffenburg (1896), which showed gradual improvements of up to 25 percent as a result of continued testing. Kitson (as described in Book & Norvell, 1922) found that during a 20-week period, typesetters with around 10 years of experience gradually improved their job

performance between 58 percent and 97 percent in response to a bonus system rewarding higher performance. Dvorak, Merrick, Dealey, and Ford (1936) reported substantial improvement."

3 Some would call a story between 7,500 and 20,000 a novelette.

4 Affiliate links.

5 Read a fascinating article from *The New Yorker* here http://www.newyorker.com/reporting/2011/03/21/110321fa_fact_goodyear

6 Wikipedia has a thorough account of the story here http://en.wikipedia.org/wiki/Like_a_Rolling_Stone

7 Here's an article I wrote about how to do just that: http://goinswriter.com/writers-group/.

8 For a list of writing blogs that you might want to start with, here's the 2012 Top 10 Blogs for Writers by Write to Done: http://writetodone.com/2011/12/23/top-10-blogs-for-writers-20112012-the-winners/

9 Or, even better, here: http://www.underground-press.org/pdf/postalrates.pdf

10 If you don't know what Scrivener is, read my review at http://thewritepractice.com/scrivener

11 These quotations were culled from the wonderful resource, duotrope.com. Find the full list here: https://duotrope.com/interview.aspx?q=10

12 If you disagree with this rule or want to know more, I'd be happy to chat with you about it. You can email me at joebunting@thewritepractice.com.

13 More about why you should create a self-hosted Wordpress website: http://thewritepractice.com/self-host-your-blog/.

14. Affiliate links.

Made in the USA
Coppell, TX
27 February 2022